Lost In The Midwest

By Wendy Weingart-Hammond

Old Seventy Creek Press 2017

OLD SEVENTY CREEK PRESS

2017 OLD SEVENTY CREEK PRESS FIRST EDITION

PUBLISHED IN THE UNITED STATES
BY OLD SEVENTY CREEK PRESS
RUDY THOMAS, PUBLISHER
P. O. BOX 204
ALBANY, KENTUCKY 42602

ISBN-13:
978-0692381724 (Old Seventy Creek Press)
ISBN-10:
0692381724

Dedication: To everyone who believes and for those who don't.... yet; "hope drops in the rain".

Cover Art by: ~ David Sanders

Born 1966 in Milwaukee, Wisconsin. David currently resides in the Phoenix. Arizona area since 1997. David started drawing mostly cartoons at a very early age, then slowly progressed into still-life and photo realism. While attending MIAD (Milwaukee Institute of Art & Design) between 1984 through 1989 his style of drawing greatly changed into abstract and surrealism. Much of his work is a glimpse into a world intertwined between dream and reality showing spontaneous bursts of creative output onto paper, canvas and digital mediums.

https://www.facebook.com/sandersartgallery/

Contents

INTRODUCTION

The poet's notion of magnitude is decidedly
distorted from that of the general population.
The almost unimaginably ordinary
details of a post-industrial existence- a Bic
ballpoint pen, a turkey roaster buried in a
kitchen cabinet three hundred sixty-
four days of the year, or an innocuous pair of
earmuffs on a winter day possess significance.
They are the treasures of our world requiring the
same care in documentation as the seemingly
more grandiose objects or events that occupy
most people's attention. It would be inaccurate
to say that as a poet, Wendy Hammond takes
time to "stop and smell the roses." This implies
some level of finality. Noticing earmuffs on a
day when they are a perfectly logical and indeed
a practical article of clothing is one thing- to
imbue them with significance, to give them mass
and gravity is quite another.

It is no small accomplishment to compose
meaningful poems in an age where the art of
nuance remains something of an anachronism.
Poems require the reader to readjust his or her
sense of magnitude. We have been told what is
"big" "meaningful" and "important" and in most
cases an anonymous pair of mass-produced
hospital slippers will not exactly fit the bill. This
isn't the case for Wendy:

When the floor gets cold
In room 453
Put her slippers on

she writes in "~What Floor." Indeed in room 453, when the floor gets cold the magnitude of these slippers has no peer. At that moment and in that space, they are simultaneously potential salvation and potential damnation for a seventy-eight pound grandmother who is close to death. This is a cosmic or religious level of magnitude, and it is found in a pair of slippers. As the reader will see in this book of poems, every object, no matter how mundane, possesses this same potential.

If the poems in this book were only about the potency of the physical world to connect to the spiritual, it would be well- worth reading. However, it would be an injustice to limit Wendy's poems to that realm despite its primacy for most people in terms of magnitude. Wendy Hammond also shows us what it's like to be a woman in America at this time in cultural history where women's bodies are manipulated to sell the most ordinary and unnoticed of grocery items- as she writes "sex sells even milk." Like the slippers in "~What Room" the milk in "~199 Sex" is a potent symbol of life, creativity, nurturing and femininity. The contradictions in the following poems are startling: freedom/oppression, sexuality/abuse, healing/sickness and often the lines between these contradictions are blurred. This is not the ordinary world, where the doctor prescribes the medication and heals the sick.

This is the real world, or as Wendy writes in "~Holes" one where *"the scales have always been lopsided."*

To read these poems, is to experience in often violently powerful and unexpected language the reality of being a woman, mother, daughter, and lover in this age of inequity masquerading as opportunity. As readers, despite the often-dark universe in which we are submerged, certain characteristics emerge that let us know that hope is out there. From the almost clinical details in "~Someone Should Teach Little Girls" where she writes:

Someone should teach little girls
how to breathe from her diaphragm
deep breaths of confidence

to the feverish adolescent sexual reminiscences of "~First Love" (a poem half-masquerading as a cautionary tale but in the end one which extols the virtue of experience despite any accompanying anguish), we are left with a complex set of responses likely different from person to person or even reading to reading, but unflinchingly consistent in hope. That hope is at times sarcastic even weary, but never truly denied and never cheapened by the unwarranted optimism or sentimental clichés. It is a hope that has been forged in difficulties and mistakes, and for these trials, it is a hope that is all the more potent- more genuinely hopeful.

As you read this book of poems you will be struck by familiar images. They are full of details that are so common that most of us let them pass without a thought like one more pair of earmuffs on a winter's day. However, each image possesses a novelty and a weight that reminds the reader of why they have become so familiar: they are necessary for survival. Perhaps the images you find will be some of the ones I have mentioned here, but likely different ones will seize each individual and do so in a unique way. As you will see, the ordinary possesses a magnitude far beyond what we are accustomed to experiencing.

Wendy Hammond's poems help us calibrate our sense of magnitude, and in doing so; they help us recognize hope in the unlikeliest of places.

Matthew Retoske

~ Lost In The Midwest

I am lost in the Midwest,
somewhere between
one great lake or another;
it doesn't matter. It is winter,
there are eight inches of snow
outside,
and my feet are cold
even in slippers.

It is gray seven days
a week. My wardrobe
cries for color. My skin
feels stale, ghostly pale
and graceful aging is
out of the question.

The snow continues to fall.
I count flakes one
by one until I get dizzy
until my thinking swells.
Until the chill walks through
the glass.

I live in fleece, wool,
and everything thermal.
A condition that reeks
of terminal arctic ice.

I am lost somewhere
in the Midwest,
waiting to elope
with the first ray of sun
that walks by.

~ Disassociation

as I load
the seventeen boxes
you escorted
to the end of the driveway,
I feel the confinement
of exactly one car length

as we transfer between
the finality of things,
I initial each line
of your checklist,
and you remind me
I hate my middle name

as I notice the changes
you've made to erase me,
the obvious things,
our dog wants my touch,
and I see you haven't yet trained her
to stand six feet away

thanksgiving is coming.
today I opened the turkey roaster
from box number fifteen
and stacked neatly inside
were the wedding napkins

bridges cross over
passing rivers, flowing streams
but sometimes
we stop in between, soak it in
see our own reflection

if we are washed clean
through water, baptized,
set free
then tears are a form of release
and rain is a means of cleansing
stimulating
growth

think of the calm of floating,
a relaxed state of peace,
the crease and ripple of a puddle
when the wind
decides to breathe

like a seedling
leaves the safety of the womb,
then blooms like a new beginning

we are given
second chances
and newfound treasures
when nurtured by liquid pleasures
when watered devotedly

they would come
sit like mannequins
in high back chairs
around tables
with square checkered boards to each side

drink burgundy wine
as Beethoven and Mozart fought for the piano

arrange their pawns into horizontal lines
sometimes black, sometimes white
a game to the left, a game to the right

they wore straight faces and serious looks
turtleneck sweaters
smoked pipes and cigars
and blew smoke into each other's minds

the pawns and the bishops staggered about
the rooks, sooner or later left their corners

and my eleven year old curiosity
studied the male aggression
contemplation and succession
piece
by piece

filled their glasses, emptied their ashtrays
and lapped up their stray thoughts
in the silence between moves

and i wondered why girls weren't invited
to play— when the most powerful piece on the board
was female

Eighteen,
I knew everything.
Lust has no power steering,
you go where ever
it takes you.
Running with the moment,
like there would be no others.
His eyes were
climbing fast,
and I was ready
for the roller coaster ride
of a lifetime.
.....*Look Mom—No Hands*

Coasting,
through love's routine
stuck in-between. Twenty-seven
without courage or choice.
Conscience has all the power,
it makes you stay
when you should go.
Turning away from the moment,
bending just to bend.
Convinced there would be
no more sudden rushes.
But still I wasn't ready
to ride
the ride alone.
.....*Look Mom—No Glory*

Flying,
with strong wings
and awakenings.
Thirty-something,
I have all the power I need
to hug the curves
and breathe.
Freedom came the moment
the mirror began
forgiving things.
.....*Look Mom—No Strings*

I am a deep royal blue
Curls and ringlets, slants
And drips
I shake my hips
And the page wiggles

He starts to read
And I plant a seed of curiosity
Word by word
Stroke by stroke
I sing for him in cursive

I doodle in the margin
An elusive spring
A thirsty flower, the art of lusting
As the tip of my pen
Spreads its wings and flies

Brushing rhymes against my thigh
Teasing hem from line
And parting
Crossing the borders of his mind
Until I'm vivid and defined

The paper lifts
As if it comes alive
And he smells my perfume
Like the mist of morning
In the heat of july

As I write him
The smooth touch of my skin
Pressing against his
With the ink of my pen
The tip of my tongue

This is a poem
Unbuttoned
Undressed
It curves and slants and drips
Down the page

She wears her hair wind-blown
wild, with a positively-me
smile, and the "not sure who
I am" child within her eyes.

Do you recognize her?
She walks upright,
a confident woman,
with firm breasts and shapely
hips and oh, yes, …thighs.
Legs a mile long and strong,
her heels dancing
to that "I Am Woman" song.

She's a real go-getter,
when the odds get better
on roaring days. But, ohhh, baby,
she likes to laze about,
and maybe pout alone.

She's a red-hot classy
down to the bone, a bit
too brassy, even sassy
when you're coming on.

So if she's PMS'ing,
it's the best thing, if you
just stay away. She's a brazen
bitch and temptations angel,
and some days even that
gets tangled, but it's okay.

It's a woman's way to gloat
or wail, float or sail, or child's play.
She'll either kiss the mirror,
or miss the mirror,
depending on the day.

~ Just Dance

poetry is dance to me
—you just dance

as if space is a lover
it moves with you
covers
then exposes
in one breath

the way a dress sways
sprays her scent in a mist
around the room

soft waves of light
make half-moons on the wall

as the rise and fall of sound
and movement
glide with rhythm, fancy feet

comes now verse
asks to dance

like when first
lovers meet
unencumbered
chemistry

— like poetry
you just dance

she imagines
if he rolled around in her
stirred slowly
toes in sand

she would thicken, turn to cream,
drip between his fingers
on his hands

stretch the moment
over August
the heat of summer
the ocean breeze

touch each other
silken mist,
then turn over, tender kiss,
please,
unbutton this
she whispers

I don't want composure
the way perfect ladies sit with their hands folded
in their laps, legs crossed at the ankle just so,
and all the hope one could ever want
fattening their smiles

they must be pretending

how did they preserve their innocence,
did they can it with the tomatoes
on hot summer Saturdays, then wait
for the lids to pop
while chatting over iced tea
and fantasies they'd never dare explore

they must be bored

working the tools of womanhood
in flowery dresses, cleaning up everyone else's
messes, lining up the Ball jars, covering up
the scars that keep them in the kitchen

canning themselves

what happens to the little girl
told to fetch the lid rings from the cellar ?

When his poems
Come down the mountain
With a ripple effect

A piece of sky
Followed by a golden haze
—I become wildfire

Wearing Chantilly lace
And the music he makes
Like bait, luring

My skirt like tumbling wind
I want to dip my toes in
Lake Cumberland

Skip stones
And write poems like him
— Ripple down a mountain

His bowed hat,
and all of that blue
tucked up under
for the under-loved,
the under-paid and the fading ones.

Those shades of blue
he's unpacking,
tunes about lacking,
those baby left me,
baby blue, blues.

He's bending notes,
slouched against a bar stool
in stained rooms
where you could peel
smoke off air.

The fog perched there,
as his belly relaxes over his belt.
And every feeling ever
felt is in his voice and dancing
in his eyes.

A man whose music
soothes souls,
rubs aching backs, and passes
the collection pail for overdue tears,
a receivable, with years of appreciation.

And he lays it down
casually like a barmaid tip.
As the harps have
a musical conversation,
and the sax refills his glass.

In twelve measures of
rain down on me
spirituality, sexuality,
defined as Chicago blues,
there are no laps of luxury.

Only overflowing ashtrays
and one guitar, bottleneck slides,
-one, -four, -five,
watery eyes and smiles.

Until closing time,
when that bowed hat
tips to the crowd,
and all of that blue
turns navy.

the picture is crooked
dust caked on its frame
streaks down the glass

to most,
it is unnoticeable

the generations know—

they try to straighten it
wipe it off,
hide their neglect

so visitors only see
the beauty

of the small child
sitting among the wildflowers

~ The Appointment

Doctor, tell me
why do the nights stir me up like this,
the room pirouettes, corkscrews,
the thunder kicks the mattress
and I walk the dark
like a scared child
crying for someone to turn on a light

Sometimes in crowded rooms
I feel out of place
like the wrong curtains
or being under-dressed,
as if the scars glow
and everyone knows
something isn't right

I dialed you
from the big black print
splashed on yellow
on a weak morning
the day January died,
because I had turned into ice,
because the night before
I laid on the floor infant-like
in front of the fire
and did not melt

So, Doctor, tell me
did I look pathetic
in my over-sized shirt
with the hurt stains
and pain slopped on the front,
when you said sit down
and there were six chairs to choose from

and I asked, is this a test

I remember speaking of vultures
of longing, of daddy,
you, with your clip board,
loafers with no socks,
scribbling my uneasiness
into hopscotch squares,
me, asking what I said
that you found important

Cramming my desperation
into a fifty-minute hour of purging,
wondering how many boxes of Kleenex
were stacked in your supply cabinet,
if I would even need them
—I doubted it

My malfunction came to you
hunched over, hobbling,
cramped with shame, neglect,
and worthlessness
—diminished

and I begged you
make me whole, a cure

and all you could do
and all you could do
was medicate me
until next Tuesday at two-thirty

until next Tuesday

~ String Beans

Perhaps
Grandma taught me
To snap the string beans
For anxiety relief

Maybe she
Knew more
Than I gave her credit for

Because here I sit
Forty years later
In the middle of it
With a bowl of
Tense green beans
And a pile of little endings
I need to throw away

On a hot summer day
In the middle of july
I split my fears
And eat my tension
Every seven times

-And I see grandma's hands
Showing mine
Breaking off
The split ends of life
One bean at a time

There are fewer
Wide open places
Less room to breathe

And it takes longer
To get there

Where you can reach
And see
And touch
Outside the box

Where we are stuffed
And smothered
Encumbered and unaware

Staring at the walls
Watching the clock
In a cubical existence
Where we've become

—Elevator music

it's not about loss anymore

it's not because the moon did a somersault
and the sky opened up
and you thought
it meant you could fly

it's not because the stars formed her smile
or because the spaceship you built
was designed for adventure

it's not about rushes, infinity,
the speed of light
or uncontrollable urges,
or even biological clocks ticking

it's not the planet you landed on
but the planet you wanted it to be

and the question remains
why you needed to travel
in the first place

now, it's about
cleaning the spots
off the rear view mirror

~ Perhaps (Two)

Perhaps
I'd sit next to you
In the quiet autumn air
In my old pair of blue jeans
With the holes in the thighs

And you'd put your hand on my lap
And pick the frayings
Like a nervous alibi
And I'd be praying you'd land
Fingertip to skin

Make music out of wind
From the poems in my eyes
As I'd lean in
Closer to your side
So I could feel you breathe

Hear my heart flutter
Like the falling leaves
And somewhere underneath
I'd tremble in color
And you'd steady my knees

In my old pair of blue jeans
With the holes in the thighs
In the quiet autumn air
Your hand in my lap
-Perhaps

I feel him pressed against me.
The first thought of the morning
is silent, yet understood.

His breath, radiant upon my neck
trickles with anticipation
under the sheets.

Our bodies feel the pulse
of desire, embrace
the motion, accept the urgency.

We reach the summit,
breathing heavy, before dawns
light finds us cradled here.

Satisfied, our bodies spoon,
We never spoke,
or opened our eyes.

~ Calvin's

Like the fit of
Calvin Klein jeans,
there's something
comfortable
about having
my hips hugged,
being pulled into.

A man, like denim
—rugged,
with callused hands,
can be hardened
and softened
by the way a woman
takes them off.

~ Brilliant Shades Of Light

The nights are getting cooler
Bring a sweatshirt
And your camera
The leaves are changing

The trees are getting ready
To strip for winter
Some of their arms have fallen off
And all their hands are trembling
As they wrestle with autumn

Clusters of mahogany, orange
And cinnamon
The cracklings of October
The scent of summer's end

A freshness in the air
You've got to breathe this in-

It's a stirring change
Of season,
When the sunset dips behind the trees
And all those trembling hands
Fight for its intensity

As day falls out of sight
With a little curiosity
You can see between the leaves
Brilliant shades of light

She summons the rain, palms
raised, painting space with her body,
crayoned in blues and greys
and shades of silver dripping,
as if she is animated,
the sky exaggerated beyond itself.
She runs barefoot, tanned
and wet, upsetting the thunder,
praising sparks of light against
final curtains.

Her chants, her wind-like callings
stir midnight into a vast whirlpool.
Light feet, and constant
fallings, she dances the fool of a rainmaker.
And the cries of her white dress
clinging to innocence, lessen.

Splashes of sin, of could-have-beens,
recoil and bend into oblivion.
Like a forgotten bed-sheet pinned to the clothesline
flaps and snaps in the breeze,
the stronger the wind, the harder the rain,
soon she is freed of sodden linen,
left naked in her pain.

Beginnings and endings
are one in the same, a bathing,
a flooding, eventually draining her.
So she angers the storm
with both arms extended, in a dance
with the dark, the lightning flashes,
the sky and black patches
of ruin.

Exhausted of all she had left to give,
all she had left to be taken,
she lays down in the puddle of
forsaken dreams,
and beads of rain
swallow her.

~ She Claims To Be A Poet

today, i decided
that maybe these words are for dreamers
or maybe the introvert
with a tied tongue and sleepy eyes

each touch, the fingertips
realize their effect

in retrospect, i find
i'm still learning how to write
still learning how to sleep
on the surface of night

where sometimes i stand outside
and howl at the moon
just to experience the feeling
of really being alive

if i spend too much time
in memory, i lose sight
of where i'm going, and i know
it will suck me dry
that's why i fidget sometimes

that's why i write

a risky state of emotion
my own blindness, sees
how brittle life can be,
and the voice,
my lack of choice in the matter

is what makes me a poet

i'm writing this poem naked
it's raining, and there's a cool breeze
at the window, parting the curtains
like a peeping tom

it's night time, the sky looks purple
and i am glowing by candlelight
subtle as a shadow
painting graffiti on the wall

the ink is dripping in streams
and i'm skinny dipping in it
flooded with emotion, moonlit,
my breathing something constant

in the mirror of my reflection
my muse is dancing,
humming something about love,
—wet with inspiration

The damn forgiven,
—because I was too easy
to eliminate,
because when I was a kid
I watched the peas for hours
then ate them cold,
because I wanted peace
and less to spit out.

Anger, dependency,
raw inadequacy,
because the fucking
know-it-alls
said sin would send me to hell.

They defined sin,
then they defined me.

Conform
said the wind,
don't open your mouth
or the bugs will fly in
and multiply
in the belly of your fear.

Imagine
how a fresh abrasion
stings when submerged in water
then shrieks from pain
when touched by air.

It is the unexplained
that draws me,
curiosity that drives me
to test our thinking,
and society that tries
to close me in.

I am uprising,
free speech and a pen.
I will write nude,
spitting peas across the room,
smoking a cigarette,
exercising what little rights
I have left.

~ Running On Empty

Today I'm running on empty
The bank account is overdrawn
Disconnect men line up at my door
At eight o'clock in the morning
With one hand out and one hand turning off the water
The electric, the heat
And the car is out of gas parked out on the street

And all of them will charge me
Penalties and fees
Another setback, another squeeze
They kick me
When I'm down
When I'm already on my knees

Collectors harass my phone
Until i have no tone left
And honestly, -it's almost a relief
As the job I thought I had
Runs a background check
To make sure I'm not a felon
Or a druggy or a thief

What difference does it make
If your credit score goes negative
Insurance rates increase
Like I'm a better driver
Or lacking a disease
Or a better employee
If I have money in my pocket

They sock it to me one more time
In the welfare line
Where I've come to beg for kindness
So I jump through hoops
Then sit and wait
Like a well-trained dog
With no pride left

I'm one woman, one income
Three kids and a pet
Living day to day, paycheck
To paycheck, in survival mode
In the frozen wind of winter
I search for a way to stay out of the cold
Put food on the table
Without selling my soul

We work our whole lives
To survive and be told
Sorry you're sick, sorry you're old
Good luck holding on to your home
Pawn your gold, sentimental things
Your rings
Things you can't take with you

All the fears and tears we hide
As our government decides our fate
Takes our rights away
And the American dream
I once believed
"the harder you worked
the more opportunity"
Is running on empty

Today
I pull the covers over my head
-Play dead
There's two cans of soup in the pantry

And tomorrow is another day

Hollowed out
Like the dead log lays its head
On a bed of sienna, rust and saffron

A white flag flaps free-spirited
And the wind sings
A tragic song

Broken limbs
Stagger about
From long falls and entanglement

As the vines to freedom feel their way in
Through the cracks in the sky

Continuance
The rotation of time

As night, or first light
Descends
Everything bends accordingly

Unlike how animals
Defend the wild
The cycle of life

We drag our dead
From the front lines
With their insides falling out

And what finds its way home
Still walking
Stumbles about —hollow

~ Clouds

i'm studying clouds again
looking for a sign
a little reassurance

for faith, light will rush through
when given opportunity

for guardian angels
floatation devices
and tails of grandpa's coat

kite strings
little girl dreams
lilacs
—hope

because sometimes
if you nudge your way through
all that blue
will lift you up

where you can see
a clear day

~ Thinning The Woods

It hung there
above a red pool,
emptied, slightly swaying
with a glass-eye frozen stare —stiff.

I remember wondering
where its insides went,
which gleaming eye sliced its center,
whose hands reached inside.

The mixture of sweat,
in-heat scent,
gun powder and blood
was stuffed up my nose.

Proud orange hats circled,
counting trophies,
already fattening their
camouflage, decorating the mantel wall.

Then came the snap,
the thud
of limp, deadness,
and twelve hands reaching.

As the tail gate
of the hearse dropped,
they secured the tag
to its ear.

And they called this
…thinning the woods

you came
when I didn't know you were coming
sat next to me, inside my dream
like you knew everything
through dark glasses

and when you looked at me
I couldn't hide
behind my bangs or my lashes
or crawl
into the holes of my jeans

no matter how guarded I seemed
you entered me
and I became your other half
and we laughed together
and slept, wrapped as one

we've only just begun
like sun rising
and I never want to leave this bed
where I belong
my head on your shoulder

if this were a sexy poem
you would want her
almost naked on the page
with just enough
to make you curious

full of intrigue
intellect and mind play,
a seductress,
a tease,
an innocent smile

and in between the words
within the pauses
where she breathes,
her pulse is quickening
as you read

and the longing of her words,
her needs, drip and run together
into streams of pleasure
and fantasy,
til she comes again
through the pen,
your hand between her knees
your finger tracing her margins

craving touch, her flavor,
lust and spontaneous behavior
weaves minds, entwines
intimacy and poetry
and leaves wrinkles
on the paper

~ Wounded Birds

You search for wounded birds,
collapsed spirits, a broken wing.
The teetering soul begging to be whole
again. It is you my friend who brings
gifts that blush a pale heart.

You bandage the wing with
simple things. Carry the rain
to wash the wound, sunshine
to warm the chill, and the moon
to put the shine back in the eyes.

And then you say,
"Start digging, take everything,
strap it all on your back
and flap, flap those wings.
Accept the load, it belongs to you."

"Become the feather and kiss the wind."

~ Clear Water

Idle
Calm
Clear water

Seeable, see-through

—Like me
When I wear my x-ray
In the daytime
In public

Dark blotches
Empty pockets
Bones and clouds

On exhibit like artwork
On a Paris street

All the people stop to stare
Soak their feet in me

Hear the empty echo
Of Catholic organ music
Two sides of a song

The ripple of the beat

And if they pray, or feel
Or reel themselves in
Through the
Idle
Calm
Clear water

Then art becomes artistry
And passersby
Hum
Somewhere
Under their skin

~ Salvaging

Bruising causes
compliance,
you begin to stop
caring, stop fighting back,

and the attacks come
less frequently.

When everything
hurts, you can't focus
on any one pain,

you become numb,
except for the blame
you inflict upon yourself.

Someone has to live
with the fist of unreason,

someone
takes the punches,
does the bleeding.

The dysfunction;
our preconceptions,

the wrong exceptions
borrowed from
generations before us,

bought by our own
inability to love ourselves.

~ The Butcher

Like prime USDA choice
he liked the way the meat
hung from my bones.

The tender parts of me
fell easily into his hands.

Once hooked,
he started looking at me differently,
as if my insides belonged to him.

Slowly he skinned,
until there were no more layers.

I hang gutted, swaying
in the freeze of
an empty physical mass.

And the slaughterer,
—he laughs.

~ Watch Me Disappear

Read me now
While I'm wounded
In the breath of goodbye
Watch, as I
Fade between the lines

Like slanted rhymes
And lost melodies
I unsing the songs I wrote
Erase the notes
And pretend you didn't happen

I didn't float within myself
And we didn't sugar coat
The truth, the obstacles
We just ran in circles
Around the rules

Like a poem when it seeps
Into the margin
We used excuses
For wanting to-
I'm unwriting, unloving,
Erasing you

-Watch me disappear

~ Music Boxes

I think of you always
with a smile and a tear,
and know it's okay.

In the quiet, I listen
and your song still fills me.

Music boxes like ours,
once wound
never stop playing.

Total acceptance, value
of time, your voice in the distance
reminds me I'm not alone.

I dance around the room,
as my other half
sits slowly spinning.

like the board
i use to scribble on
except now the writing
is more concentrated
painting the trim
of a january sky

the same shade
—just more precise
so not to bleed
into the horizon

a charcoal smudge
foggy and unclear
drips down
beyond the skyline

and i nudge myself
with wonder
as if the vault of heaven
might open

flow over
like i do when i get wordy
or when i'm on a rampage
with a poem

—i could be erased

the eye
of astonishment
blinks with disbelief

lifts its head

confesses
slow and careful
makes me wonder
who is listening

keeps me grounded
makes me able
to glisten in the glow
smell my daddy's apple tobacco

and find my way back home

~ In A Small Church Tucked In The Woods

They placed him in a box,
not unlike the one he lived in,

except now you
couldn't hear him
pounding to get out.

They displayed his picture,
in a brass frame, so we couldn't see
the rope burn around his neck.

They sat, with disbelief in their laps
in the front row like his and her towels.

The Reverend spoke of seventeen years
that he knew nothing about.

I sat off to the side, cried, then smiled.

So, you found yourself today,
walked right up to your reflection
and there you stood,
with all the should-have's,
could-have's and would-have's
puddled in your eyes.

A few crow's feet,
salt and grey streaks,
to remind you
it's not nineteen-seventy-nine anymore.
You've spent years
closing doors and hiding.
Compromising,
learning indifference wears an
ugly bathrobe
and keeps its chin low.
Life's been constant
undertow.

No carriage comes to carry you off,
no sun sets easy on a broken horizon.
It's a slow admission, fear
and crying when those
Cinderella eyes confess,
self-sacrifice leaves a terrible mess
on the glass.

Time pushes and moans
on the bathroom door,
screams a few foul words
before it bangs again.
The air stiffens, bends in a new direction.
This is the last moment

of tight-lipped prevention.
The quiet adjusts,
reflects, sits down
with its best friend conscience
and discusses the outcome.

Eyes wide open
you push yourself closer
to the woman you are.
Your fears stare back,
and in a panic attack
you're forced to see,
the mirror, that twelve year old girl
hating her body, an old woman
complaining about rain.

Behind shades you've drawn,
in the bathrooms where you
cry alone, you stand barefoot
on ice tiles, middle-aged, naked
to your own cold smile,
shaking
because something inside you
can't continue faking it,
something within you is still alive,
and you make up your mind
—the breaking stops now.

It's in the transposition,
innocence becomes maturity,
acidity finds forgiveness,
and as you pass by your
new reflection,
there is birth of solidity,
and life begins.

~ Til Kingdom Come

you taught me control of emotion
like management of the family budget

the lesser of feeling
the cheaper macaroni and cheese
might please you

the tightness between
expression
like a stranglehold
cuts off my air

my bloodstream full of Novocain
I can't feel if I'm there

and I wonder who you see
roaming the castle

a carbon copy of the perfect wife
tongue-tied and hassle-free
barefoot and dancing in her sleep?

oh, what a blind man dreams
til kingdom comes undone
and his majesty is left
alone in the palace

—unaware

Blue capped by orange
atop a silver base,
my thumb presses
red plastic and ignites
the night.

There are some things
you can do better in the dark.

A white tube-like cylinder
slim, 100's length,
stuffed with one of my addictions,
droops from my lips.
I watch the air suck
my tension into the blackness.

Inhale,
satisfy the urge to break down
each thought into one deep toke.
One acceptable form
releases the torment.

Exhale
the affliction, the clouded moments,
and admire the way they fold
themselves around each other
before they fade from view.

There are some things
crutches are good for.

Sometimes, you will find me
smoking in the dark
alone,
smoldering the night.

~ Conclusions

when you know
something's missing,
you know it by a touch
you're not sure you want
anymore,
and you find yourself un-listening
drifting toward yourself,
flying out the window

he says i'm gone somewhere
and he can't find me,
—i avoid his eyes
so he can't see where i am

maybe, i've changed my priorities
like when an old dream resurfaces
and takes on more importance,
or maybe i'm just bored
feeling fenced-in again
maybe i'm still angry
over all the things we've been
and all the things we're not

but i know something's changed
in my stare off in-space spot
where i contemplate
direction
and search for answers

when I'm losing sleep
because my dreams are sneaking up on me,
guilty of
feeling more complete

without him

this is when you know—
something's missing,
you know it by a touch
you're not sure you want
anymore

my father's voice
folded me in half
as mom folded towels
into threes

starched and stiff
it hung there
facing the same direction
as his dress shirts

I felt buttoned up
the way I was taught
to fasten the top securely
so the collar would stand-up straight

his tone wrinkled the room
she stacked her thoughts
with the clothes
then hid them away like dirty laundry

as I
continued to iron the air between them
in silence

China sat and looked pretty
Her beauty so becoming
Her delicate pattern
Her cup full of hope
Always overflowing

She paints the daisies yellow
Always yellow splashed on blue
With little specks of green
To symbolize something new
And a few faint curly q's
Along the wave of her rim

She's been chipped
And bruised by him
I see it in
The fading color
Of her eyes

She folds her fragile hands
Her stomach tied in knots
And tries to wipe the spots off
The petals of a rhyme
She never forgot—

He loves me?
He loves me not.

I cannot reach my breath
when I am under you. Yours
is pressing into me, and mine
hangs motionless a few feet away
monitoring the way light
travels across your back.

Your body hard against,
could crush me
with the weight of hunger.
The headboard
like gunfire into the wall behind us.

You press my wrists into the mattress
and hold them there,
like lockdown
before the coaster drops,
the anticipation
before my belly flies off.

My body the sponge
feasts on your sweat.
The scent of sex
the circumference pendulant
around us.

As the sounds of cascading
harmonize,
my eyes —call out
from the peaks of apogee,
and we are released
simultaneously into a climactic float.

Then come the whispers,
slow and sluggish,
into the valley
of gentle breezes
as the drops and puddles of us
dissolve into the sheets.

~ A Woman's Song - A Sonnet

a woman's lips will sing of strength and love,
down winding roads, in dreams of wishing wells,
upon the wings, in cloudless skies of doves,
her home is where the apple blossom dwells

in fields of common men, her heart is true,
each babe held tightly to her breast, she keeps
for beauty smiles in every morning dew,
and on each child's face she tucks to sleep

her hands are gentle, tender like the wind,
can mend the threads of time, with just one kiss
and even when she crumbles from within,
the world around her surely blinked and missed

the woman picks up faith, and dusts it off
for she is strong as stone—and cotton soft

She used to dance in her stocking feet
on the slippery gymnasium floor
on Friday nights, with a disco ball light
spinning around sprinkling everyone
with white dots, like chickenpox
for teenage heartthrobs.

And the band played Color My World
for a paint-by-number class
on where to place your hands.

Giggles and wiggles, clicks
of curiosity, flickers of imagination
huddled in bubbles in the hallway.

Hormonal squirts of soda pop,
live bullets lined up in touchdown stance
near the girls bathroom.
Chaperones with magnifying glasses
checked for hikkie outbreaks,
unlocked lips and handcuffed hands.

And everyone was feverish
with adolescence.

~ Out Comes A Growl

I hear the bear,
his pounding footsteps
charge for the cave.

It's happening.
I can feel it, smell it
the way a storm steers in,
not unexpected, just late.

The wind accelerates,
leaves separate from the trees
like when baby cubs set out
to misbehave.

The slave of his tension may eat me.
Grizzly and mean,
rough day.

Will his claws hesitate
if I undermine my existence
hold my paws behind my back.
Taste like honey,
go down easy, avoid
sudden attack.

Until finally, he's satisfied…
sleeping heavily

and somewhere in the darkness
—out comes a growl.

~ Mother May I

Mother may I
Bounce off the walls today
The way you did when
Things went crazy

I feel weathered
Beaten down
Spun like a ball of yarn

What harm could I be
If less of me was available
For the taking

If all apologies
And sacrifice lost power
And everything just stopped

And instead of breathing everything in
I'd exhale slowly,
Focus,
Spin time more to my liking
Discover who i am again
Become self-satisfied

Mother may I
Rest my eyes

Curved
Like a woman
Shaped to please
The human eye

You want to run your fingers
Along her body
See where she's ticklish
What ripples her breathing
Dip your toes in

She is calm today
Full of simple man's fish
A comfortable rowing rhythm
Slow and easy

The warmth of sun's reflection
Like a mistress
A twinkle of light on her surface
Still excites

A man of contemplation
Baited and ready
Awaits the catch of the day
Steady,
Steady

Such a teetering effect
A stimulating sensation
She is a tease
But she gives him what he needs
Asks nothing in return

His Sunday afternoon lover
Covered with evening light
Whispers the words
" —go home to your wife"

a heart-shaped jewel,
delicately scarlet,
born of a lonely flower

the plea
of an undying hunger
contemplates,
clings to the vine

its succulent taste,
enticing promises,
invite me

picked from many,
the perfect berry

bliss awaits

balancing
in the palm of my hand,
caressing
with my thumb
and forefinger
slowly,

slowly,
I raise to my mouth
gently cup my lips
around
heaven's fruit

my tongue anticipates
a bursting,
an eruption,

the splash

a rivulet of juice
drips down my chin

You knew.

I knew.

This
could be ignited
instantly,
with barely a flick
of reason.
I am living
the spontaneous season
in which
moments come
and I take hold
full force
blazing.

The temperature
is rising
wildly hot,
sparks intensity,
fingertips between us
tracing the curves
of uncontrollable urges.

I have seen us
rolling on the ground
trying to extinguish
the flames.
You on top of me,
me on top of you
—on fire.

He has a hard-on for life.
Makes love to it like a woman,
an ambition he cannot deny.

Sips twilight like expensive Cabernet,
breathes it in, swirls the moment
and relishes the bouquet.

Unjust as life can be
he sets the madness free,
and I am envious of his talent.

~ Red Shoes

I am anxious
because you are in the room
but it is crowded
and busy

everyone appears to be normal
socially interacting

but I am not exactly what you see

behind my ladylike smile
I am role-playing an erotic fantasy

under my dress
I am panty-less

and my own impatience
excites me, as I watch you
mingle

~ Less Of Us

there's less of us
to hold on to
more fences to climb
more walls

time wore us like it had purpose
gave us fragile eyes

somehow we got trapped
below the surface
fell in-between the lines

and the moments that brought us together
hide in the shadows
under big sweaters
and show their faces less often

we both own coffins
for the bitterness to rest in
but now and then
the dead rise
with cold gazes like mannequins

and we get caught in their resurrection
an infection no penicillin can cure

because the reality is
—we are less than the way we were

~ My Third Sunset Today

it's been over forty eight hours
since i've slept
and i'm not feeling tired yet
actually, i almost feel wired
or twisted or on fire or something
all complicated, all conspiring

as if i can take each worry
and teach it right from wrong
maybe make a song out of it
find a new direction

like when i'm planning a comeback
from the dead, from the self-made prison
cells of my regret
where sometimes the bricks on the wall
start to move
with the punches
and i've counted them all
a hundred times over

what is today,
i can't remember
it doesn't matter, it's just passing over
like the smoke from my last cigarette

and i'm sitting here, with the quiet
watching my third sunset
today

and i don't know my way
—and i don't have all the answers
yet..

~ Evolution

if you believe
in the possibilities
of an upswing
—in knowing
there's a familiar tickle
coming down

you'll pump your legs
a little harder,
push a little higher
toward places you haven't reached
somewhere off the ground

and the sound of your own breathing
will become familiar as you soar
constant, rhythmic, —freeing

each lift, the motion more

the flight, for the thrill of flying
no limits in your view
each change
each truth, inspiring
the sky, a clearer blue

each breath of wind
a gust of faith
each high, each lift, each fall

and the beauty
is in knowing
you can see above it all

with each ascent
there's a turn-around
a fresh breath of love
and the security of

—a familiar tickle
coming down

me and winston-salem
fill the sky with smoke tonight,
watching the rest of you
stretch to wrap yourselves around the moon
and in the distance of broken light
spots and streaks of repented sacrifice
strip themselves of life

and you believe
you will be replenished
if you ask forgiveness

such starvation, thirst and hunger
cannot measure
against deprivation of spirit,
the solitude and molestation
of innocence

and our children still believe
in the man in the moon,
dishes running away with spoons,
and all convictions that make us foolish,
because we teach them this

each raised arm, each eye gazing upward
demolishes the concept
that any of us are really alone,
and in this interaction, contact
with unknown catalysts,
we cling to heroes
who aren't heroes at all

we grow miles tall in our own disbelief
that we are anything more than
—this

a large emptiness
trying to fill each other

~ Charades

You got more
than you paid for.

Unwilling to unmask
the numb, under-thumb
existence
you allowed me.

I swallowed hard,
as you showed off your possessions.
No one mentioned
I looked uneasy,
the squirm of my feet
when you claimed to be successful.

As your creation,
the decorated me
was attached to your sleeve
like your favorite cuff links.

How dare I think
your performance shallow
fake bones, plastic smile
and perfect teeth?

I speak now,
out of necessity,
without permission or a script,
equipped with the stink of you
on my skin,
the residue of where I've been

and for your entertainment,
my voice ten times

the strength
of Chicago wind,
each line rehearsed,
I impersonate the woman
I want to be

As I take back the role
of control, self-esteem,
I draw the final curtain,
dim the house lights,
and give myself
a standing ovation

~ An Inspiration

perhaps it's raining there
i wonder how you're feeling
if you're dreaming at this moment
of a sunnier day
or if you're locked away somewhere
feeling sorry for yourself
the way i do sometimes
on rainy Sunday afternoons

perhaps you're surrounded
in bad company,
wishing you were someplace else
anywhere, —maybe with me
finger drawing on the window pane
watching the rain, warm and cozy
by the fire
snuggling in its glow

perhaps you're with a friend
reminiscing of good times
tending to your needs, drinking
a glass of wine and smiling,
surprised you still can
with all that's on your mind
but smiling just the same

perhaps you're sleeping
sprawled out on your bed
with sexy little fairies dancing
in your head, and the background
sounds of a distant whisper
composing the melody
to keep you warm

perhaps you've become
a poem

~ Grandpa Jake

grandpa jake
i make music with words

i heard you played the accordion
traveled the country with a band
had many women,
a few families you abandoned

i wonder if you still write songs in heaven
—or is it really quiet, like in catholic church,
or waiting rooms

maybe i'm too soon in asking
but that much peace could drive me crazy

imagine, if you knew me
like a familiar melody
we could spend our time listening

tapping our feet
to a sweet genetic rhythm,
only you and i could make

grandpa jake, i understand—
the music was the reason
you had to keep moving

—now, how do i find
a soothing
lyric for that

here is the suitcase
full of regret
the bets i've placed
on sure losses

the heartbreak
and soul ache
and everything i'd take back
if i only could

it's heavy and bulging
and i'm overflowing
losing my grip
trying to carry the load

old photographs
loved one's passed
lost love and missed chances
expand and breathe within

as the cold sets in
-i hold my breath
like winter wind
un-passing

The bergs stand,
isolated statues,
ballplayers on the diamond
among waves foaming
at the mouth.

The bird lady comes
wearing blue ear-muffs
carrying a bag of stale bread.

Flocks of gulls
swoop in around her
like she's their long lost mother,
a recruiter or the water boy.

Her over-sized purple gloves
homerun the crumbs into the crisp wind,
and thousands of stiff wings
look like Yankee stadium
with everyone clapping.

The tracks will blow over
and the sand will wear
a clean white jersey
as winter holds onto this season
with a record breaking average.

~ This Night, This Music

You are like
moon dance
and being near water,
and I am a creature of night
submerged.

Your voice, the season
of purple skies,
five a.m. fevers,
sweat on my brow,
breathlessness.

I've been chasing
constellations
with a butterfly net,
re-designing the universe.
Tonight I named a star for you.

Tonight, I listened
and your words drew new meaning
out of a tired art form,
left my skin dripping
from an almond bath.

Once, in a dream
I imagined I was air
pure as my innocence,
clear and invisible.
Surely, I do not exist.

Yet you
bring me to this page,
mirrored, surfacing,
gasping for language
explicitly for your ear.

And in our sameness,
I concede.
I swim nude, I sleep nude,
as darkness hangs above,
I see specks of light.

You tempt this night,
this moment,
with elegant dance
and the music
of water.

We don't always find
what we want in one package.
Sometimes the wrapping
is misleading,
and the contents
half empty.

After we push the peanuts
to the side,
and remove the stuffing,
there is only a fraction
of what we expected.

Fifty percent is not enough.
Potential is not what we search for.

~ What Floor

When the floor gets cold
In room 453
Put her slippers on

Call the family
The doctor is coughing
Grandma won't be home next Christmas

January rattles bones in the basement
Elevators ting empty

Hospital beds are full
Of abandoned mannequins watching TV
Last good-byes
Void eyes
People learning to release

A slow cry away
Below freezing degrees
The snow makes days seem still enough
For a thousand years of peace

She's having trouble breathing
Could the angels' come
Please...please...
Sit with the man at the end of the hall
The nurse ignores his calling out
He's afraid dying is contagious

With a sting and a tear
The way medicine pinches air
Potent and bitter strong
It won't be long now

Kneeling in the corridor
Begging for an injection of faith
Trying to find safety in numbers

She's only seventy-eight pounds
Barely breathing

When will the doctor come

When the floor gets cold
In room 453

Will someone put her slippers on...

~ Hangover

I awake, my head
floats above my pillow
I try to think
with soggy brain cells
everything looks crooked
I drank too much of you
over-indulged last night
impulsive like when
Marshall Fields has
a 50 % clearance sale
we drank shots of the moon
until it was empty
kissed each other's hunger pains
swam naked in delirious waters
animal instincts surfaced
with appetites the size of Texas
two bodies joined
on the floor, in your bed
the kitchen, the shower
I can still smell you
my skin tingles
how do I return
to my ordinary existence
without this tell-all
smile on my face

~ In Real Time

If I can love you in real time
Not tomorrow
Or time past
Or times when betrayal took me for a ride
I'd rather ride on the back of your Harley
And watch the sky turn purple
At four a.m.
Feel the temperature rise against my face
Whisper on my skin
Wear lace stockings to tease you

If I can give you the best I have left
Without resistance
Or personal neglect
Or fall behind time as a victim
I'd be a fool to lose one moment
Of the sky dripping, us kissing
In a crowd

I want to scream out loud
In a free-fall from a cloud-like float
Somewhere above it all
Painting lavender walls with my body

I've never known anything steady
But I'm ready to believe
You can weaken my knees
Without withering me
Stroke my thigh, look up my skirt
And maybe, this time
No one will hurt
No promises broken

If I confide,
Speak of things I've never spoken
Feel all emotion
—And do it in front of you
Allow myself to get accustomed to
Reaching for you in my sleep
will I be safe in your keeping

will I be safe in your keeping

In whispering thoughts and sheets of white,
the vision comes, enters me suddenly, without
a sound, brings the ceiling down to touch
my nose, and all the words begin to sing in harmony.
It is a piece of memory, a distant dream, a fantasy,
a fear unseen, and everything that could ever be
tiptoes across the page. A sudden rage of broken-ness
strips off its dress and walks naked across the room.
It is doom, an unending tune that pounds behind
my left ear. A tear that wilts the paper, a masked invader
of my soul, and yet, I still search, still cry at night, still
cover my eyes when my blues get too bright, and all
the actions that I take are fated to shake the spirit
down, wander around with mouths agape, with promises
slipping off tongues of hate, and all others who refuse
to see, words can heal, words can breathe
new life into all who take the chance, to glance beyond
their own safe worlds, turn left outside the gates
and travel toward nameless, faceless states, where all that
is defined as strong, and all that is forgiven as frail,
empties me then fills me again, and leaves a paper trail.

~ The Drowning

I drowned these words last night
filled the bathtub
then tossed them in,
watched them try to swim
only to find the sides were slippery,
and there were no ladders.

I knelt down, leaned over,
took my forefinger
and held them under,
then I'd let go
and watch them bob up and down.
Some sank, others floated
some kicked and splashed around.

Words like "trust",
"optimism" and "love" were the fighters,
others gave up easily.
I watched "compassion"
try to save "hope", and
"pain" sank to the bottom.

I opened the drain
delighted to hear
that slurping gurgling sound
as all were sucked away.
Don't ask me to explain
how they sustained themselves
and landed on this page.

there's a place
where the sky dips down
and swallows everything around it
brilliant it seems
when such visual dreams
crawl under the sheets
cool and peaceful

there are plenty of days
when the rays of the sun
reach to retrieve
what's been strung all over
and pieces of me
naturally
run off in all directions

as if the colors I've become
are a rainbow smeared
across the sky
almost childlike
erratic and unexpected

the way my fingers
finger paint
a background blue
the conflicts, the eruptions
of my life

~ Idle Stands

the symptoms are simple
you move sideways
instead of forward

you lower your head
balance fear
as if it were something
you could stabilize

each scale
at the angle for learning
each decline transmittable
to those who dare near

as the slant of yesterday
drops off
—calling
you reposition your feet
because falling is out
of the question

so you pick up your bones
strap yourself down
and hope you'll be saved

but somehow you're always
left jagged, faded,
shifting foot to foot
waving in the wrong direction

as the runaway train
you want to run off with
keeps running

If I take you in little doses,
if I can maintain a steady pulse
and flutter only in slow motion
then maybe I can recover.
Maybe this entire lover idea
is weak in its knees
and only a concept that is
pleasing to old
romantics.

I suppose there is plenty
of time to reflect
and I know, I think too much
and neglect the moment.
But sometimes, a side-step
gets in the way, and it's
hard to walk around
each other.

Give me a minute
to regain my composure,
place my heart back
in the file folder stuck
in-between things-to-do
and things-I've-done.

I'll get back to it someday
when I have more time,
when I get my glasses fixed,
so I can see it and touch it
and feel it
—for what it really is.

~ A Dangerous Lullaby

Melancholy midnight
Drifting through
A blue room, the mood
Of the song
Soft and moaning

I am composing
A long night, broken light
Inching its way
Over piles of poems
Over miles of heartache

There is no faking it
When I'm overflowing
I never wrote a thing
Without knowing where
I had to go, —to get it

Into the core of love
With no resistance
Into the hole in the wall
The depths of
A lonely darkness

Tonight the music
Is my essence, like a mist
My breathlessness
Exposed because
There is nowhere to hide

When extremities collide
In a blue room, the mood
Of the song
Soft and moaning
Is a dangerous lullaby

I float through the air
dandelion fuzz
clinging to a noon breeze,
watching my fingernails grow,
hair curling under my arms.

I've learned to be stingy,
hoarding my time,
rolling
my eyes at the angry past.
Dismissing the day from demands,
I crawl from the bed to the chair
and back.

Lonely poets
are no different from me, licking
paint, crocheting cobwebs,
a leap off the ledge
from twenty stories.
They could fly
or sleep forever.

I still exist
in laden ashtrays,
the hollow soda cans, crumpled Kleenex.

I practice sadness
like piano. Tomorrow
I will compose lyrics.

~ This Room

The carpet is rusted, flaking.
My stubborn aching crawls around
under the pad. So comes this
lazy winter, a splinter from the
past.

This room drags me under
into consequence, into the
clutter, through the mess.
I am cold, and I am alone,
and there is the mirror,
and here is my fear
grinding itself in my bones.

I search for the faucet,
to silence the uneasy drip,
the burning blood
that slips and puddles within
and around me.

One room of confusion,
won't settle down
to rest, I cry
for a transfusion and
extend my arm.

a thin film coats the surface of
midnight
as lightly as a bed sheet
hides each layer
of sleeplessness,
delirium oozes onto a black sky
drips through the confines of space
and the lace Priscilla curtains breathe
heavy

it almost sounds like rain

some things stay the same—
deep sleep never comes,
buried alive
I gasp half awake, half aware

the ceiling looks down
and I stare back
counting down minutes by digital blinks

the clock's eyes are red
and I think I might disappear
if I stay unconscious
—clearly so

I know all dreams are forgotten by
morning
repressed or neglected
either way, gone

gone the way grandpa's body
fit into that small urn,
gone like ex-husbands, broken dolls
and used razors

I stretch, roll over, get up on my knees
then crawl toward daybreak
like flame against heat,
fold the creases
of strong vs. weak

and trance-like, step to my feet
and sleepwalk
through the day

I imagine, she was soft once
as her sandpaper hand extended
toward me, her defeated voice
asked for a cigarette. I gave her
the pack.

Roaming the heart of South Bend
at ten a.m. hunting garbage cans,
through office trash for anything
worth cash, a meal, a bath or a bed,
I wonder if she's eaten.

A bulging war green duffel bag
strung over her left shoulder,
a chip or a boulder on her right.
Yet there was a sweetness
in her voice, a timid smile,
something kind but lacking
in her eyes.

A hardcore life, an empty expression
-disgraced, no safe place
to rest
Jungles like this—
are all over the U.S.
I imagine, she was soft
-once.

~ Guitar

I know you're sleeping
But I've been thinking
About full moon's and your guitar
Playing in the background
How every time I try to run
I turn around to find you
And a safe place to land

Your hands hold my virtue
My goodness, my passion, -the fire
We create in the wee hours of the morning
When the world sleeps
-We are exploring
Fingertips creep, and we are deep
Into each other

In intimate song
Harmonizing along the curves
And creases
Under the sheets
Where we completely
Un-complicate
The act of love

And I wonder if
You're dreaming of me, my hair
Falling down, your arms wrapped around
Me for safe keeping
I know you're sleeping
But I've been thinking
About full moon's and your guitar

Heartstrings
Play dead love songs
On a broken guitar
All the stars flicker out
All the blood
Drains from my heart
And forms the pool I drown in

~

I liquefy, I melt like music
Dripping down the sides
Of a moonless sky
And I erase your voice
With the charcoal of your eyes
All the words, all the times
You said nothing to save us

~

There is enough darkness
For me to hide
Draw a new dream without you
Wish on stars I cannot see
Beyond the midnight moon
Buried in the night
Of letting go

~

My eyes cover the holes
Of weeping widows
The wind sings from murky shadows
In misty, melancholy echo's
Lost black notes
With no hope to compose
Salvation

~

This time
Night has fallen hard
Broken hearts, rough edges
And in the dark, the pitch black dark
I try to erase
The tragic art
Of loving you

~ Stacked On Flatbed Trailers

Mexican's work the fields
stacked on flat bed trailers
a fork in the road
blinks yellow lights
slow down
but do not stop

churches mark the corners
—so territorial we are
hypocrites praise each other's goodness
and try to recruit the rest of us
into believing we are better than
just because we attend

police officers patrol
the marinas of the prosperous
as the yacht club watches out the window
and a river away,
one overpass
a downtown so down
full of black and brown misunderstandings
cries at night
for one more chance

over the bridge
under the lid
of conservative
live two and a half
latch-key kids
and a dog that wants to run away

condom is a household word
like Cascade, or Tide,
dispensed like hand soap
in restrooms,
piercing noses,
tongues, belly buttons,
an expression of who we are,
painting our bodies with tattoos
portraits of our individuality,
wearing our sexual preferences
like an overcoat,
underwear is outerwear,
breasts displayed like trophies
silicone symbolism,
young girls feeling
Barbie Doll pressure,
anything is in
everything is out,
a need for lack of conformity,
shaving, not shaving,
hair color chosen
from a box of crayons,
we all want different,
sexual acts in public places,
we stare
like virgin catholic girls,
who read Cosmo in their closets,
we advertise
using hard bodies,

sex sells
even milk

~ Old Movies (Previewing)

It comes down to this;
a flicker of light, one long
breath, one deep sigh,
and no compromise.

The purging stopped
twenty minutes ago
when the air froze, and the room
stood numb between us;
when all the fuss settled
down and sat on the coffee table
alongside the Cable Guide
and the remote.

Our eyes got fuzzy,
the fight in us tired, and
the volume died down
while emotions flipped
like channels
in the background.

Until all that remained
were two sets
of empty eyes
staring at a blue screen.

i can't enter a public library
in any town, anywhere
without first pausing
at the entrance

and i almost see him
out of the corner of my eye
propped against the porch wall
reading himself to sleep

and i remember
how he said to me
"i manage to keep adequately
warm"

but its january or july
i can't remember
and i'm not warm
although i'm dressed for the weather
just knowing where he sleeps

we were like two old souls meeting
for the first time
connected at the eyes
and i know he's been on both sides
of these walls

you'd think within the archives
of these hallways
we'd have learned
somewhere among the ages
and all the pages of our wisdom

how to bring him in
from the cold

I used to watch them
sitting on the bleachers
rocking, drooling,
shaking, slurring their cheers.
"Hey batter batter, hey batter batter."

Sometimes I'd look up
toward the barred windows,
and wonder
who they didn't let out
to watch the game.

The teams would come
from all around,
take their places on the diamond.
The patients whistled
if they could, and whistled
even if they couldn't.

I think I was ten,
watching dad hit home runs,
holding back my tears,
trying to understand their smiles,
as coke ran down their chins,
and popcorn missed their mouths.

"Hey batter batter, hey batter batter!"

~ Breakable

She was twenty eight,
—twenty eight.

They found
more pieces of her
than she had years.

Fragments of bone,
thrown about in less
than a blink.

Her broken-ness
scattered
along the tracks.

Plastered
flesh against steel,
flesh against wheel,
flesh against
living.

She stepped between
the scissors hands,
hypnotized by the eye
of an instant exit.

Jimmy had long hair
And my daddy, who wasn't afraid
Of anybody,
Was scared of him

Jimmy loved rock and roll,
Screaming guitars and alcohol,
Played bass guitar and trumpet,
Wrote me songs and poems

Jimmy was a musician,
A hard-core condition,
I remember one Halloween,
He dressed up like Gene Simmons
From the rock band "Kiss",
—I liked to kiss Jimmy,
Run my fingers through his hair,
Feel his tongue squirm around mine
With his trumpeter lips vibrating

Jimmy was older than me,
Much more experienced,
Daddy would have built a fence around me,
But I would have climbed over it
Just to be with Jimmy

Daddy grew eyes in the back of his head,
Every time Jimmy and I sat in the den
Pretending to watch TV,
His hand on my knee,
And daddy forgetting his magazine,
Then his glasses or anything
So he could re-enter the room

Jimmy liked to squeeze my boobs
When no one was looking,
I felt sneaky, and let him fondle
The new-found woman in me,
And in exchange, he'd put my hand
On the bulge of his blue jeans,
And I'd squeeze him back

Daddy would have had a heart attack
If he'd known I was responsible
For Jimmy's rising,
-My hormones soaring
Out of control.

Jimmy and I explored
All the bases, one by one,
He was patient, loving me,
As I headed toward home plate,
Daddy hated Jimmy

It took a year and half before I gave in,
Before I gave Jimmy my virginity,
And turned into a woman
In the back of a borrowed Chevy Van,
The night the band played
Kiss songs and we drank beer

I snuck home, spent hours looking in the mirror,
Making sure Daddy wouldn't see
What I gave Jimmy the night before,
That I loved another man, —not necessarily more,
Just differently than Daddy,
Jimmy had long hair

~ He Comes

When the pages are full he comes,
after an old rage has settled in ink.
After she's emptied herself
until there's nothing remaining
except shadow;
a few provincial phrases
hanging from the chandelier,
and some tears puddled on the
dining room table soaking up the napkins.

He's late, —too late for her.
If he would have come twenty years ago,
if she had only known he was coming
then she might have been able to stop
the running, the chasing after.
Hanging her heart out
only wore it down faster.

He comes now, after the story
is told when she has coiled
within herself and faced
her own fullness and failure,
—that nothing is certain.
No floral fantasies
that once led her down dark alleys
overjoyed and afraid and alone.

He comes after the last chapter,
appendix and afterword,
beseeching. When there isn't
any laughter, nothing left to share,
and the only look left in her eyes
is indifference.

With a tired sigh she turns
her cheek to the pillow,
closes the book;
turns out the light.

For those who wipe tears from their shadow...

Day One ~ Desperation

I stepped into the world of Celexa,
I wore a black cloud, concrete shoes,
And a sloppy expression.

A wingless bird,
Asleep.
Incapable of breathing in.

Day Two ~ The Headache

My head swelled,
An over-stuffed garbage bag.
Someone took all my pens and pencils
Poked holes in my brain.
Everything leaked out.

No words today.

Day Three ~ Pale

Balance the chemical imbalance.
But the scales have always been lopsided.
Mood elevation sooner or later crashes
Like a 747 when the engine malfunctions at 30,000 feet.
It's a long fall.
Makes staying asleep appealing.

Pale and tired.
Only one fit of rage today.

Dirty dishes accumulate in the kitchen sink.

Day Four ~ Suspended

My head is floating above my body.
I am detached.
Uncertain change is possible.
Elevation, daydream
Salvation, complicated thinking.
Nausea worse than morning sickness.

Forgot to eat.

Day Five ~ Choice

Shower or go back to sleep.
Someone said life was out there.

The sun was brilliant today
— i noticed.

Read a section of shakespeare
With my sunglasses on.

I was a sponge.

Day Six ~ Unfocused

I watched as my mind
Took a tour of its contents.
Paths of destruction, corners of doubt.
Boxes stuffed with fear, seals broken.

I wiped tears off my shadow's face.

Forgot to take out the trash.

Day Seven ~ Feeling

The sky spit rain.
Hopelessness came strolling
By the window again, chin heavy,
Wearing a slouch, carrying memories
In its backpack.

Wet with emotion, i cried for the first time
In over a year.

This is good.

Day Eight ~ Light

Lifted to the surface,
I saw over the privacy fence.
There were living things, —living.

Lilacs always take me home.
I inhaled.

I am still afraid of empty houses,
Spotlights,
And crooked smiles.

I almost felt safe with the nightlight.

Day Nine ~ Calm

The birth of calm.

I settled in the soles of my shoes.
The ground didn't move,

Only a distant rumble.

The edge was silent for a change.
The shapes of clouds intrigued me.
There wasn't anyone to blame today.

I crawled out of my grave and cleaned the dirt
Out from under my nails.

Day Ten ~ Able

Able to listen to silence.
A slow lifting fog, the runway.
Cleared the rubble and witnessed the storm
Dismiss itself from my body.

Blue took on new meaning.
The sky was brilliantly complex.
Each swallow went down easier
Each blink, less awkward.

I sat alone on the back step
And didn't feel lonely.

Day Eleven ~ Beginning

A beginning.
Washed off my war paint.
The realization
There isn't a cure,
But i am able to fill the holes
With acceptance.

Answered the phone.

~ The Annulment

Take it back?
But I loved him more than life itself.
I wore a white dress with a fifteen-foot train,
had three-hundred witnesses
and a video tape.

Pretend we never
lived with roaches
made six dollars an hour,
had all used furniture
and a new baby bed full of anticipation.

He never stayed out all night,
and I didn't overreact,
or puke in the kitchen sink
at 5 a.m. with morning sickness
and the smell of sticky sausage patties
on my hands
trying to make his breakfast.

We didn't
make love so passionately
the people downstairs
beat on the ceiling,
and the neighbors had a cigarette.
He never slept inside of me.

No doors slammed,
None of our china
shattered against the wall.
I didn't clean it up.

The day our daughter was born,
he wasn't out drinking with friends

while I greeted visitors
and made excuses for him.

Tell me
he didn't find a strange bed,
he never came home and told me
he loved her.
And I never had anything to prove.

I spent twenty years dreaming of,
over a year planning to be,
ten years living as
— his wife
and now you want me to pay you
to un-bless us, to tell me
it never happened?

God knows this happened.

~ My Feet

I look at my feet
They are ordinary feet
Except usually I paint my toenails silver
Like stainless steel

And maybe that's to remind me

I look at my feet
And I see those steel toed boots
Holding 220 pounds of angry
Pinning me to the kitchen floor

It was a day of final straws, endings

I look at my feet
And I see pieces of the oven door
Shattered all over
Crystal and pristine

And I can see my reflection

I look at my feet
A burning candle
Thrown against the glass patio doors
Hot wax streaks everywhere

And I know it will take weeks to clean it up

I look at my feet
And they look back at me
And we both see the bruises
Of that day

My feet turned and ran away, and I followed

I look at my feet
They are ordinary feet
Except usually I paint my toenails silver
Like stainless steel

And maybe that's to remind me

~ Breaking Stride

I'm doing okay
with the everyday things.
Dragging my ass out of bed
each morning,
—functioning.

Enter stage left, an actress
in funky platform shoes,
choosing her stride, the role
of someone more whole
and aligned.

I've done the routine.
I've been somebody's whore,
somebody's queen, somebody's
everything
—nothing,
and stuck in-between.

I'm learning the walk
all over again, how to wiggle
just right, get the spunk in
my talk,
sleep through the nights.

Won't tie my tongue
like a dirty shoestring…
I've stopped tiptoeing around
uncomfortable things
and breaking stride.

~ Breakfast

I want breakfast
served on the side
of a morning fuck, steaming
coffee, sweaty sheets,
a soft touch

breaking smiles
like daylight sun,
silk unlaced, clothing undone,
the slow slide
of a hungry tongue exploring

bring day to life
under covers, under fed
a taste, a bite
a twist of light, blankets tumbling
off the bed

until we bubble
then turn hot,
until the coffee in the coffee pot
turns bitter,
and the alarm clock
—sighs

the moon sits on a slant
halfway
between you and me

can you hear my breathing
like wind through trees

its early in the morning
yet
i haven't been to sleep

i spent the night wading
the shoreline of a dream

now four a.m. is fading
into contemplative state
as i wait for you

holding all my truth
moon-kissed and witnessed
by another night alone

i search the starlit sky
for a place to cry
because i feel it in my bones
coming on

the missing you, the wanting to
dissolve the distance

and i listen for your voice
in every moan of night
reach for your hand
and pray i might

lay down beside you
on a blanket on the moon

close my eyes
and blink you true

~ Night Moves

~ I

I take no prisoners
I wear all the faces of my shadows
And their clothes
To blend in
To the corners they stand in
Huddled, humbled old souls

The bones of dead muses
Buried in the basement
Like ghosts clanking poems
And if you listen close enough
To the undertones
They will enter you
Like the manic light of moon
Slices up the room
Into brilliant hiding places

~ II

Late at night
When the trains come through
When I think of you
Passing through me

My green
Green eyes
Upon your navel
Your poetry
I wonder if you know
I'm still listening
To the rumbling of the tracks

You left on me
And their vibration

And I'm still writing poems
Of explanation
Hope drops in the rain
Waiting for the train
To stop moving

~ III

In the dark, in the white
Of a black angels eyes
Two moons shine
And I am drawn into
A liquid light
Calmed by this night
This calling

I crawl under wing
Without questioning
Where we're going
If we're floating or falling
A slow weightless lift
Through a transient mist
Into morning

~ First Love (Two)

among the old boxes
—somewhere

next to my high school yearbooks
and prom pictures

are the songs you composed
to soothe my heart

and if i close my eyes
and imagine you— sitting
—all hands and guitar

i can still hear the music
you made for me

the music i gave
my virginity to
and the lyric that witnessed it

—but sometimes
no matter what we do
love isn't enough
to brave the difference

and the melody gets lost
within the silence
of letting go

i could still love you
—but i won't

~ Someone Should Teach Little Girls

Someone should teach little girls
the mirror is her friend. To bend
out of a flawless state of mind.

Barbie dolls come from a perfect mold.
Womanhood does not. Shapes and sizes
are only motives people use to define.

Someone should teach little girls
how to breathe from her diaphragm
deep breaths of confidence.

Shadows and tall men are not meant
to shade. Walk into the sun, make your own
light, and then learn how to belong to it.

Someone should teach little girls
to dream without limitations.
Doors only open, if you open your eyes.

There is a Ken on every corner
who will try to make you feel less than.
He is a waste of time, —a compromise.

Someone should teach little girls
her body is a gift, to be given
only willingly and of free spirit.

Someone should teach little girls
how to love, how to be loved,
how to give it and how to take it.

I will, yes, I will teach my little girls
they are more than…

~ Poem star

He enters this poem
Tall dark and handsome
An instant attraction
I can't deny
Like gravity, his eyes
Pull me inside
And I get lost there

I come revealed
Open and honest
Ready to feel
-Something
His kiss stops my breathing
And my heart
Skips a beat

Our bodies meet
Our fingertips
In-between our margins
On top of the covers
Under the sheets
Under the pleats
Of my dress

All tease, all tongue
His soft lips
We taste, we please
I move my hips
To the rhythm we create
To the magic
That we make

All man, his hands
Ignite my passion
Pull my hair
Hold me down
And take me where
This poem explodes
Upon the paper

if he knew
how i contemplate
-stay up late thinking
string myself along
write a song about it
while i'm sinking
into him

how it all begins
with a caress of wind
a stirring inside
as i close my eyes and imagine
the music we make
-takes my breath away
this rhythm

how it plays me into sunrise
softly moaning
at the wonder of it all
half-asleep
still dreaming
stirring underneath
cool sheets

daybreak spinning
through the room
his song in my head
i wake-
with music on my lips
kissing morning

I'm thinking about you again
Caught in the middle of a slow curve
Singing with the radio

Windows down, my hair blowing
Driving the old back roads
With a tickle in my belly and I know it's all your fault

I gain speed and the gravel flies
As the sun almost melts my thighs
I imagine your blue eyes riding shotgun in my life

I clutch the steering wheel
I can't deny I feel
Tingles I thought had died a long time ago

I breathe in, like getting high
On human pheromones
Your scent on my pillow

And I wonder if you know
By the green of my eyes
I drive and dream and drive, and fantasize

And the more I drive
The clearer I see
The possibilities

And I'm thinking I might let
My heart race for you
And go wherever you take me

I told the voice to go away
kicked her out
like my ex-husband
burnt her words in the ashtray
page by page
rage by raging rage

until I screamed
—and there was no sound
until ash covered the silvery base
and laid there
still like death
and she wasn't breathing

smothered
by the heat of paper emotions
crooked devotions
and everything cheap
as a Bic pen

if she speaks
I will burn her words again
if there is a resurrection
I will light us both afire

i used to read
McKuen, Langston and Jack
by the spot of a flashlight
under the sheets
with Sexton and Plath
when I was sixteen
and vulnerable

when my innocence
was intact, waiting to find
direction
a better definition of naïve
fewer pre-conceived notions
something to believe in

conform or bend
into an acceptable shape
for the sake of fitting in

i began to see
our worldly measures
weren't so important after all
.

it was words
positioned in brave stance
beatnicks, quick fixes
hungry addictions
for language
and rage splattered
like graffiti on the overpass

scribbled by tall men
and brave women
with huge voices

and determination
to change the way we see

i hid under bridges
where you could hear clearly
the sounds of movement
and imagination

like a troll

i sat
with my voice in my lap
and secretly spied on the world

this is a cage,
these are the bars,
these are the scars from trying
to escape, here are the scratches,
the holes and patches,
the claw marks on the pantry door

this is the cellar, the storeroom
for misfits, down in the basement,
musty and damp, there is the clock
with a sticking tick, and here
is the lamp, burnt out blue
this is the view, it's a picture
of you in a mason jar,
here is the mirror above the basin
where you are, here is the cover of an
empty book, torn out pages,
a startled look

this is the stage
where you read your rage
to a dead audience, here are
the palms pressed to the glass
of a false defense, there
is the lid holding you in, forbidding
air to enter, these are the gasps,
here are the traps set
to keep out the users

here is the salt to rub in the wound,
the broom in the corner
to sweep it away, this is
the truth, the masquerade
and this is the way, the
way you fade.

this is the jar, placed on the
shelf, lined up in rows, a facade
of faces, these are the traces
of what remains, this is the
rain, these are the stains,
all are preserved, properly
sealed, and labeled
"human aches and pain"

here is the hand that put you there
next to the one who ripped out
her hair, across from the one
sitting cross-legged,
barely there, rocking

here come the others flocking in,
more jars, more healing coffins,
a place where you harden
and soften, then kiss yourself goodbye,
this is the dying, these are the ends of
tight ropes, here are the hopes
lost and forgotten, everyone
copes in isolation, everyone copes

this is the sound of desperation
slipping and dripping
down the water pipes, these
are the days, these are the nights,
and here is the shattered lighting,

this is the mirror you're
fighting, and these are
the souls hiding behind the cold
bars, the lost stars, —the lost stars
in jars
…in jars
……in jars

.

www.ingramcontent.com/pod-product-compliance
Lightning Source LLC
Chambersburg PA
CBHW071223090426
42736CB00014B/2946